SOUTHERN MIDDLE SCHOOL

4053182007

Graphing energy
333.79 SOL

REAL WORLD DATA

GRAPHING ENERGY

Andrew Solway

Heinemann
LIBRARY

Chicago, Illinois

© 2009 Heinemann Library
a division of Pearson Inc.
Chicago, Illinois

Customer Service 888–454–2279

Visit our website at www.heinemannraintree.com

All rights reserved. No part of this publication
may be reproduced or transmitted in any form
or by any means, electronic or mechanical,
including photocopying, recording, taping, or any
information storage and retrieval system, without
permission in writing from the publisher.

Edited by Nancy Dickmann and Rachel Howells
Designed by Victoria Bevan and Geoff Ward
Original illustrations© Pearson Education Ltd
Illustrations by Geoff Ward
Picture research by Hannah Taylor

Originated by Modern Age
Printed and bound in China by Leo Paper Group

13 12 11 10 09
10 9 8 7 6 5 4 3 2 1

**Library of Congress Cataloging-in-Publication
Data**
Solway, Andrew.
  Graphing energy / Andrew Solway.
    p. cm. -- (Real world data)
  Includes bibliographical references and index.
  ISBN 978-1-4329-1519-3 (hc) -- ISBN 978-1-
4329-1534-6 (pb) 1. Power resources--Juvenile
literature. I. Title.
  TJ163.2.S655 2008
  333.79072'8--dc22
                          2008008457

Acknowledgments
The publishers would like to thank the following
for permission to reproduce photographs:
©Corbis pp. **5** (epa/Christophe Karaba),
10 (Bettmann), **14** (Stuart Westmorland),
20 (Sygma/Igor Kostin), **23** (Reuters/Javier
Barbancho), **26** (Ashley Cooper), **27** (Roger
Ressmeyer); ©FLPA p. **9** (Frans Lanting);
©Getty Images pp. **17** (ChinaFotoPress), **18**
left (The Image Bank/Ed Honowitz), **18 right**
(Science Faction/Louie Psihoyos), **24** (AFP);
©Science Photo Library pp. **4** (Pasieka), **12**
(Richard Folwell); ©Still Pictures p. **6**
(VISUM/Thomas Pflaum).

Cover photograph of Kurobe Dam, Japan,
reproduced with permission of ©Getty Images
(Sebun Photo/ Muneo Abe).

Every effort has been made to contact copyright
holders of any material reproduced in this book.
Any omissions will be rectified in subsequent
printings if notice is given to the publishers.

The publishers would like to thank Harold Pratt
for his assistance in the preparation of this book.

Disclaimer
All the Internet addresses (URLs) given in
this book were valid at time of going to press.
However, due to the dynamic nature of the
Internet, some addresses may have changed, or
sites may have changed or ceased to exist since
publication. While the author and publishers
regret any inconvenience this may cause readers,
no responsibility for any such changes can be
accepted by either the author or the publishers.
It is recommended that adults supervise children
on the Internet.

CONTENTS

Some words are printed in bold, **like this**. You can find out what they mean by looking in the glossary, on page 30.

BUSY DOING SOMETHING

What is energy? If we say people have lots of energy, we mean they are always rushing around, doing things. When we talk about energy in science, it is actually very similar. Energy is the ability to make things happen. Anything that moves has **kinetic energy** (movement energy). Heat is a kind of energy, and so is electricity.

Something can have energy even if it is still. A snowboarder standing at the top of a snow slope has **potential energy**. He is not moving right now, but if he steps on the snowboard he will come whizzing down the slope. A match lying in a matchbox also has potential energy. If you strike the match it will burn, producing heat.

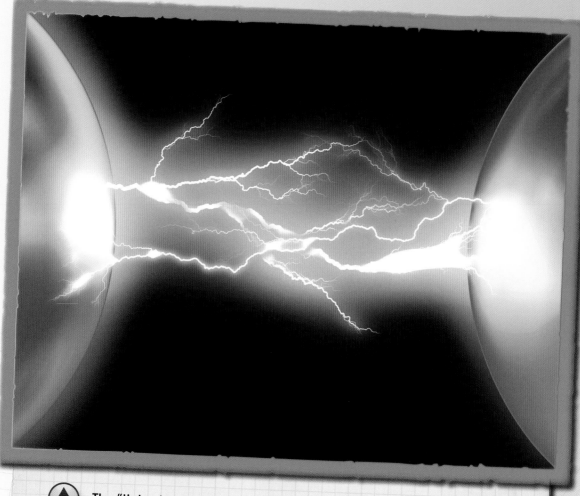

The "lightning bolts" in this picture are electric sparks. Electricity is the most important source of energy in the modern world.

 Before a race, athletes such as these cyclists eat energy food such as pasta or rice. This builds up their energy reserves.

Energy needs

In the modern world we use large amounts of energy. Most of this energy comes from three **fuels**: oil (petroleum), coal, and natural gas. These are known as **fossil fuels**. Fossil fuels are excellent fuels because they contain lots of potential energy. However, there are problems with fossil fuels that mean we need to use less of them and find new sources of energy.

Graphs and charts

Learning about energy involves a lot of **data** (information). All through this book, there are graphs and charts to help understand this information. Charts and graphs are ways of displaying data visually. They make it easier to see patterns in data and help to make sense of complex information.

There are over six billion people in the world. Among all of us, we use a huge amount of energy. In 2005 the total world energy use was 500,000 million megajoules (see box below). That is enough to power eight billion washing machines all day and all night for a year. And the amount of energy we use goes up each year. So, why do we need so much energy? What do we use it all for?

How we use energy

Just about everything we do uses energy. In homes and offices we need energy for lighting, heating, and cooling. We also use electricity to run everything from washing machines to computers. In factories we use energy to manufacture (make) **goods**. The raw materials to make all these goods come from industry—places such as **mines**, **oil refineries**, and **chemical plants**. Another big use of energy is for transportation. Cars, trucks, trains, ships, and aircraft all need **fuel**.

Energy and power

Energy is measured in joules (J). For large amounts of energy we use megajoules (MJ). One MJ is equal to one million J. Power is a measure of the amount of energy produced per second. It is measured in watts (W). For example, a 60 W light bulb uses 60 J of energy every second.

A city at night blazes with energy. The lights of the world's cities are even visible from space.

Line graphs and pie charts

A line graph can show how world energy use changes over time. Time in years is shown on the **x-axis** and the amount of energy on the **y-axis**. The slope of the graph is steeper on the right. This shows that energy use is rising more quickly now.

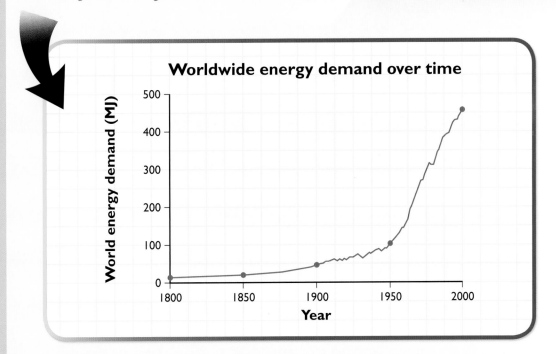

A pie chart can show how the whole of something is divided up. This pie chart shows how our energy use is divided. The biggest slice of the pie shows where the most energy is used—in industry, to produce raw materials and make goods.

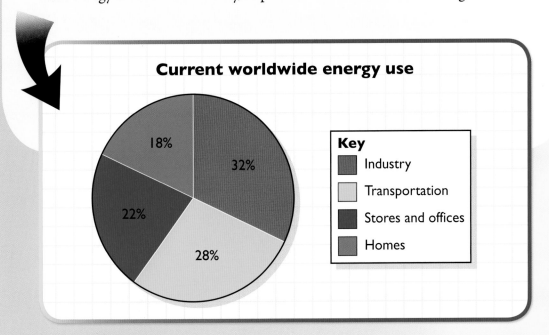

Most of the energy used for transportation, for heating, and for powering large machines comes from **fossil fuels**. The engines in cars, trucks, and other vehicles run on gasoline, diesel, or other types of **fuel** made from oil. Heating can be fueled by gas, oil, or coal. Most other machines we use are powered by electricity. But electricity is a type of energy itself. How do we produce it?

Electricity from steam

Most of the electricity we use comes from power stations. In power stations, electricity is produced by **generators**. Turning the giant generators requires a lot of energy. Most often, this energy comes from burning oil, gas, or coal. The fuel is burned in a furnace to produce steam. Steam at high pressure is then used to turn many-bladed propellers or fans, known as **turbines**.

This diagram shows how a fossil fuel power station works.

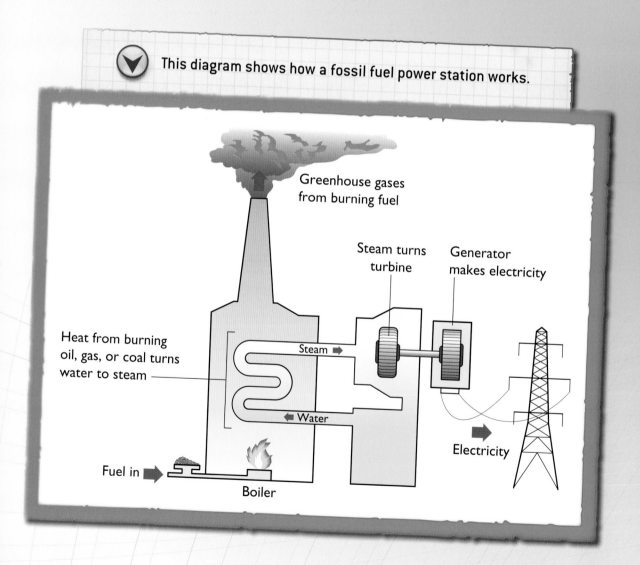

Greenhouse gases from burning fuel

Steam turns turbine

Generator makes electricity

Heat from burning oil, gas, or coal turns water to steam

Steam ➡

⬅ Water

Fuel in ➡

Boiler

Electricity

Biggest in the world

Another way of turning the turbines to generate electricity is to use the power of rushing water. Electricity generated this way is called hydroelectricity. The world's biggest power stations are hydroelectric power stations. The two biggest are at Itaipu Dam on the Parana River in South America, and at the Three Gorges Dam on the Yangtze River in China. The generators at the Itaipu Dam can produce up to 12,600 **megawatts (MW)** of electricity—enough to power over six million washing machines. The Three Gorges can produce over 18,000 MW when all its generators are working.

The hydroelectric generators at the Itaipu Dam are among the most powerful in the world.

World electricity generation by type, 2001

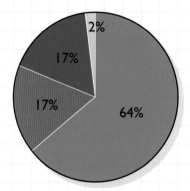

2%
17%
17%
64%

Key
- Fossil fuels
- Nuclear
- Hydropower
- Other renewables

This pie chart shows the main kinds of energy used to generate electricity. Fossil fuels make up the biggest slice, so they are the main energy sources. We use less hydroelectricity and nuclear power.

FOSSIL FUELS

Oil, coal, and gas are called **fossil fuels** because they were formed millions of years ago from the remains of dead plants and animals. Most of the world's coal was formed around 300 million years ago, when huge swampy forests covered most of the land. As the trees and other plants died, they sank into the swamp. Over millions of years, a combination of pressure and heat turned the forest remains into coal.

Spindletop Hill

For hundreds of years, oil was used only for lamps and as a **lubricant**. Coal was the main **fuel**. All this changed in 1901, when drillers on Spindletop Hill, near Beaumont, Texas, hit oil. Spindletop was not the first oil strike, but it produced huge amounts of oil—more than all the other oil wells in the country combined. This led to a huge boom in the oil industry. It was the beginning of the age of oil.

 The Spindletop oil well was a "gusher"—it shot oil out in a great fountain.

Oil and gas formed in the lakes and seas. The remains of dead sea creatures drifted to the bottom and gradually built up in large **deposits**. As with coal, a combination of heat and pressure turned these deposits into oil and gas.

Where fossil fuels come from

Most fossil fuels are found deep underground. Coal is obtained by digging it out of **mines**. Oil and gas are extracted by drilling into the ground using a very long drill. Once the deposit is reached, the oil or gas may rush to the surface, or it may need to be pumped out.

Bar charts

A bar chart is a type of graph that helps to compare groups of things that are not directly related. This chart shows the 10 countries that import the most oil. (Import means to bring oil from one country into another.) The vertical **y-axis** shows how many gallons each country imports per day. The taller the bar, the more oil the country imports. One oil barrel holds about 160 liters (35 gallons) of oil.

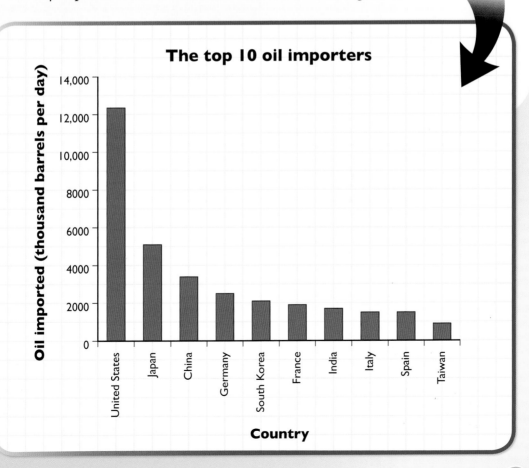

The top 10 oil importers

So, what are the problems with **fossil fuels**? One problem is that they are not **renewable**. Fossil fuels took millions of years to form—we cannot replace them once they have been used up. In the past, there seemed to be an endless supply of fossil fuels. However, more recently it has become clear that the supply of fossil fuels is limited.

How long will fossil fuels last?

Experts do not agree about how long fossil fuels will last. An average prediction is that oil could last another 40 years or so, gas another 60 years, and coal about 200 years. However, long before they run out altogether, we will reach a point at which the amount of fossil fuel we can produce each year will be less than we need. If we do not find alternative energy sources, we will not be able to produce enough energy for all our needs.

Fossil fuels are not always easy to get to. This oil rig is drilling for oil far out in the ocean.

Looking at fuel reserves

The best way to look at **fuel** reserves is by using a bar chart. A bar chart is a good way of comparing information among groups. In this case, the chart has three bars for each area of the world—one for oil reserves, one for gas reserves, and one for coal reserves. Within each group of bars, you can compare the reserves of each type of fossil fuel. The Middle East, for instance, has plenty of oil and gas reserves, but almost no coal (so little that you cannot see it on the chart). You can also compare one fossil fuel across different regions. For example, **Asia Pacific** has the world's largest coal reserves, followed by North America and the **former Soviet Union**.

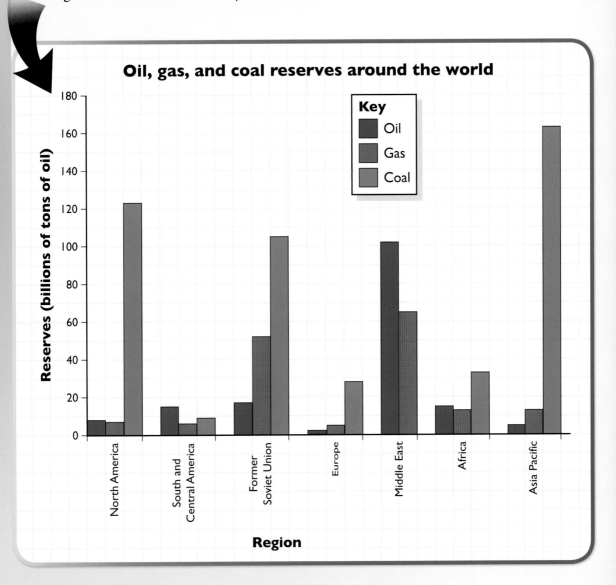

Oil, gas, and coal reserves around the world

Finding a replacement for oil in the next 40 years is a big enough challenge. But in fact we need to replace all types of **fossil fuels** as soon as we can. This is because burning fossil fuels causes other problems.

Carbon dioxide

When fossil fuels burn, they release several different gases into the **atmosphere**. The most important of these is carbon dioxide (CO_2). Most scientists agree that carbon dioxide is having an effect on the world's **climate**. Overall, the world is getting warmer. **Ice sheets** in the Arctic and Antarctic are melting, and in some warmer regions, farmlands are turning to desert. Climate change is also probably causing more extremes of weather, such as hurricanes and rainstorms. The changes are caused by the greenhouse effect.

 Parts of the Arctic are warming 10 times faster than elsewhere. This area near Canada's Baffin Island should be sheet ice.

The greenhouse effect

When sunlight hits Earth's surface, some of it bounces off into space. Carbon dioxide helps to change the atmosphere so that less sunlight can escape into space. When there is more carbon dioxide in the atmosphere, more sunlight is absorbed, and the atmosphere gets warmer. This is called the greenhouse effect, because it is similar to a greenhouse trapping the sun's energy.

Stopping climate change

We urgently need to cut down the amount of carbon dioxide we produce. There are two main ways to do this. First, we can reduce the amount of energy we use. If we use less energy, we burn less fossil fuels and produce less CO_2. Second, we can find different energy sources that do not produce carbon dioxide, to replace fossil fuels.

Multiple line graphs

This double line graph shows how two things change over time. It has a **y-axis** on each side. The blue line shows worldwide CO_2 emissions, measured in billions of tons on the left y-axis. The red line shows the average world temperature, measured in degrees Celsius on the right y-axis. (0° Celsius equals 32° Fahrenheit.) Both lines go up, showing that both temperature and CO_2 emissions are increasing.

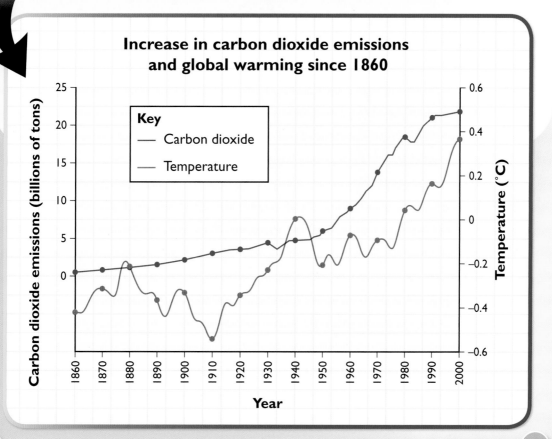

Increase in carbon dioxide emissions and global warming since 1860

Key
— Carbon dioxide
— Temperature

SAVING ENERGY

If we use less energy, we put less carbon dioxide into the **atmosphere**. People in **developed countries** use more energy than those in **developing countries**. People in developed countries drive cars, take vacations abroad, and buy lots of manufactured **goods**. People in developing countries often get around on foot or on public transportation, grow their own food, and buy very few goods. This means that if a developed country cuts energy use by 5 percent, this saves much more energy than if a developing country cuts energy use by 5 percent.

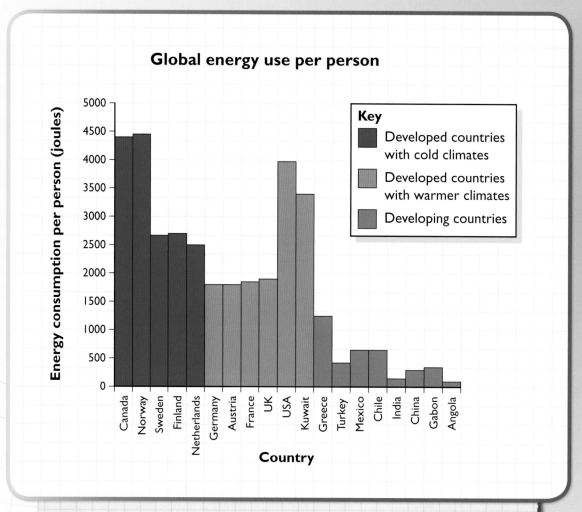

Global energy use per person

Energy consumption per person (joules)

Country

Key
- Developed countries with cold climates
- Developed countries with warmer climates
- Developing countries

 This bar chart compares energy use per person for a range of different countries. The blue bars show developed countries in cold **climates**, where more energy is needed for heating.

 The SIEEB low-energy building is a large office block in Beijing, China. It stays cool in summer and warm in winter with minimal heating or air conditioning.

Low-energy buildings

One of the main places we can save energy is in buildings. Most buildings waste large amounts of energy. We use energy to heat them when it is cold and to cool them when it is hot. However, we could save much of this energy if we **insulated** buildings better, so that heat could not get in and out as easily. Buildings can also be designed to take advantage of natural heat and light from the sun. This cuts down on heating and lighting costs. Fitting solar panels and wind **turbines** can also help (see pages 22–23). These can heat water and produce electricity for the building.

Techno-windows

Most of the heat lost from a building escapes through the windows. However, modern windows can greatly reduce heat loss. Some types of high-tech triple-glazed windows can reduce heat loss through a window by more than 50 percent.

Another way to reduce our energy use is to make machines more **energy-efficient**. This means getting them to do the same amount of work with less energy.

Manufacturers of cars and other vehicles have been improving **fuel** efficiency for many years. For example, modern airplane engines are much more fuel-efficient than in the past. There are also energy-efficient refrigerators and washing machines for the home. One new type of washing machine uses steam jets instead of water for washing. This saves both energy and water.

Recycling waste

Recycling waste can save energy. It takes much less energy to recycle materials than to extract raw materials from the ground. Recycling aluminum, for example, uses 95 percent less energy than producing it from scratch. Metals are especially good for recycling because they can be recycled again and again without affecting the quality.

Many people now recycle paper, glass, and cans. Some types of plastic can also be recycled. This kind of recycling saves energy and also reduces the amount of household waste.

 Recycled building materials can save lots of energy. These "bricks" are made from recycled cans.

 Modern low-energy light bulbs use about a third of the energy of conventional bulbs.

Standby power

Many televisions, computers, and other electronic devices do not switch off completely when you press the off switch—they go to standby. This means that they use electricity while doing nothing. Most devices on standby use as much power as a low-energy light bulb (10 to 15 watts). This adds up to a significant waste of energy.

Stacked bar charts

This table and bar chart both show the same **data**—how much energy is wasted in standby power in different countries. The bar chart makes it easier to compare the different countries. The section colored red in each bar shows the amount of electricity wasted by equipment on standby.

	UK	USA	Japan	Germany	France	Netherlands	Australia
Total power use, per home (W)	750	1000	500	440	543	370	462
Power wasted on standby, per home (W)	75	50	60	44	38	37	60

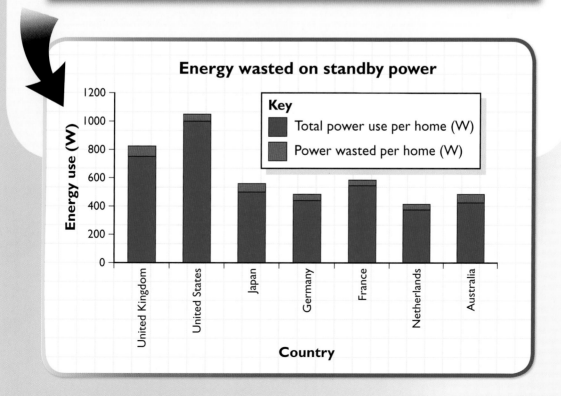

Energy wasted on standby power

Key
- Total power use per home (W)
- Power wasted per home (W)

Energy use (W)

Country

RENEWABLE ENERGY

The best way to cut down on carbon dioxide is to find cleaner alternatives to **fossil fuels**. Hydroelectricity and nuclear power are two ways of generating electricity that do not produce carbon dioxide. Could they become alternatives to fossil fuels?

Water power

To make hydroelectricity, a dam is built across a river to form a reservoir. Water from the reservoir flows down a large pipe. The fast-flowing water can be used to turn a **generator**. Hydroelectricity is useful, but it does have disadvantages. Large areas of land have to be flooded when a river is dammed, and places below the dam get less water from the river. It would

be hard to generate lots more energy using hydroelectricity because the best dam sites are already in use. However, small-scale hydropower could be used in many areas.

Power from atoms

A nuclear power plant gets its power from a reaction that splits **atoms** of a **fuel** called uranium. This generates lots of heat, which can be used to make steam and turn a generator. It would be possible to build many more nuclear power plants. However, the waste fuel from a nuclear power station is **radioactive**, and it stays that way for thousands of years. This radioactive waste is dangerous to humans. Keeping it safe is a huge problem that has not yet been solved.

 A big concern with nuclear power is the danger of accidents. In 1986 the nuclear power plant at Chernobyl, Ukraine, exploded. Many people died, and radioactive gas was released into the air. The site is still hazardous today.

Water power in use

Sometimes one graph does not tell the whole story. The bar chart below shows the hydroelectricity generated by the world's top 10 producers. However, the pie charts for the United States and Brazil show hydroelectricity as a percentage of total electricity produced. Although both countries produce nearly the same amount of hydroelectricity, in the United States it makes up just a small part of the total.

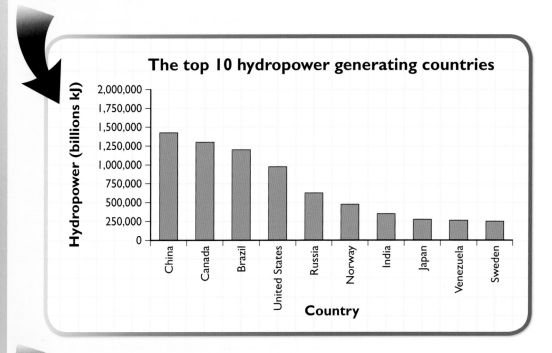

The top 10 hydropower generating countries

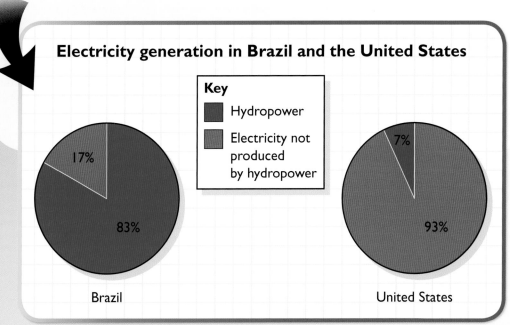

Electricity generation in Brazil and the United States

There are many other sources of energy around us that we could use to make electricity or to do other work. At present these types of energy do not contribute much to overall energy production. However, wind power and solar power are growing rapidly in importance.

People have been using the force of the wind to provide energy for many years.

In the past, the turning sails of a windmill provided the power to grind grain into flour. Today, windmill sails have been replaced by giant propellers that turn electric **generators**. In some places, wind farms with whole fields of wind generators produce as much electricity as a **fossil fuel** power station.

The falling cost of energy

Line graphs are useful for showing how things have changed over time. They can also predict what will happen in the future. This line graph shows changes in the cost of wind energy. The cost of wind energy is falling, and it may fall further in the future. Wind power has already fallen to around the same cost as fossil fuels. People are more likely to use alternative energy if it is cheap.

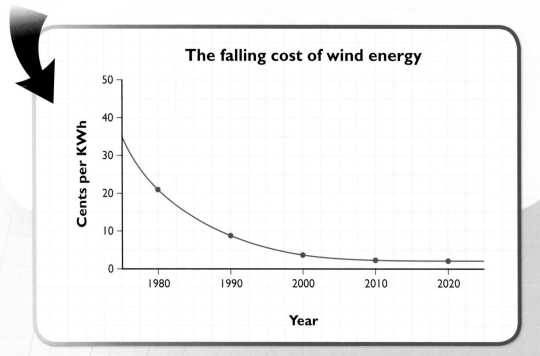

The falling cost of wind energy

Solar energy

There are two types of solar power that are growing rapidly. Best known are photovoltaic (PV) panels, which turn sunlight into electricity. These can be used on the roof of a building or in large "farms" that produce electricity.

The second type of solar power is solar thermal power. In a solar thermal power station, mirrors are used to focus the sun's heat onto a liquid and produce steam. The steam can then be used to power a generator.

 This solar thermal power station is in Seville, Spain. The huge array of flat reflectors focus the sun's energy onto the top of a high tower.

For cars, trucks, and other types of transportation, we need **fuels** that we can use instead of gasoline and diesel. The most promising replacements to date are biofuels.

Biofuels

Biofuels are similar to gasoline, diesel, and other fuels, but they are made from plants. Biofuels burn to produce carbon dioxide, like **fossil fuels**. However, the plants they are made from take up carbon dioxide from the **atmosphere** as they grow. So, when the biofuels are burned, they are only releasing the carbon dioxide they took up while they were growing. Some carbon dioxide is produced in the process of producing biofuel. For example, carbon dioxide is produced when making fertilizers and weed-killers that are used to help grow the biofuel crop.

 One new kind of car already being made is the hybrid. A hybrid car uses a combination of an electric motor and a small gasoline engine.

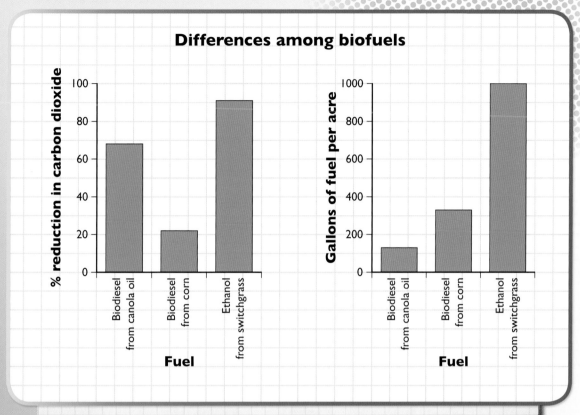

Differences among biofuels

 This bar chart shows that different biofuels perform very differently. Bioethanol from switchgrass produces far less CO₂ than bioethanol from corn. It also produces far more fuel per acre than the other biofuels.

Types of biofuel

The first biofuel to be widely used was a gasoline substitute called bioethanol. It has been made in Brazil, from sugarcane, since the 1970s. Bioethanol is also made in other countries, usually from maize (corn).

Another type of biofuel is biodiesel. This is made from plant oils such as canola oil. Bioethanol and biodiesel cannot directly replace gasoline and diesel in car engines. However, car manufacturers could adapt current cars to run on these fuels.

Fuel cells

Fuel cells produce electricity like batteries, but they run on fuel, usually hydrogen or methanol. Fuel cells could be used in the future to power electric cars and other vehicles. Fuel cell cars have already been built, but at present fuel cells cost too much for them to be used in ordinary cars.

ENERGY FOR THE FUTURE

Researchers have been developing alternative sources of energy for over 30 years. So far, all forms of alternative energy have some drawbacks. So, how should we plan for the future?

Planning ahead

In the near future, we will need to use a mix of many different types of energy. Wind power, solar thermal power, and biofuels are the most promising alternatives for power stations. We will probably also need to use other sources of energy such as nuclear power. Biofuels and fuel cells could be used in transportation. Small photovoltaic panels will probably be widely used on individual houses. Water and wind power could also be used locally on a small scale, as well as in power stations. We also need to use energy-saving building techniques, more **energy-efficient** machines, and better ways of **recycling** waste.

 The Bedzed housing development is a group of houses and apartments near London, England. All the houses are zero-carbon—this means that overall they produce no carbon dioxide. This is an example of how all houses could be built in the future.

 One way for nuclear researchers to produce fusion is to fire high-energy bursts of laser light at a tiny pellet of **fuel**.

Further into the future, we may be able to develop other sources of energy. One area scientists are researching is nuclear fusion. This means getting power from hydrogen, using the same process that the sun uses to generate energy. If we can get it to work, fusion could produce enough clean energy to solve all our energy problems.

Fuel from pond scum

Algae are tiny plants found in water. The green scum on ponds is one kind of algae. Some algae naturally produce hydrogen, and researchers are trying to increase the amount they produce. Other algae are very oily, and researchers are looking at using this oil to make biofuels.

CHART SMARTS

We often get important **data** (information) as a mass of numbers, and it is difficult to make any sense of them. Graphs and charts are ways of displaying information visually. This helps us to see relationships and patterns in the data. Different types of graphs or charts are good for displaying different kinds of information.

Line graphs

A line graph is best for showing trends in connected information. If the same thing is measured at different times, the results are best shown on a line graph. In this graph, we can see that since about 1940, energy consumption has generally grown very quickly.

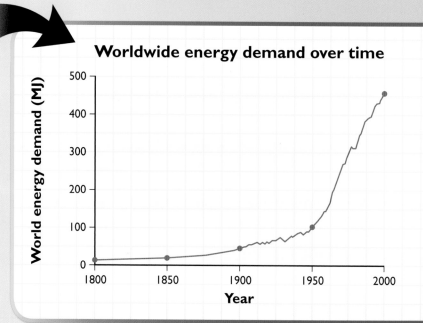

Pie charts

Pie charts are the best way to show how something is divided up. They show information as different sized portions of a circle. They can help you compare **proportions**. You can easily see which section is the largest "slice" of the pie.

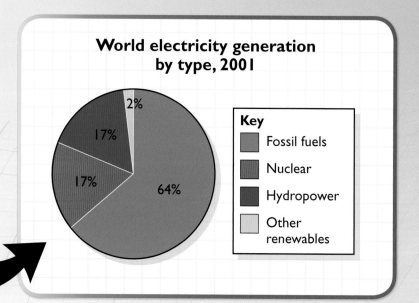

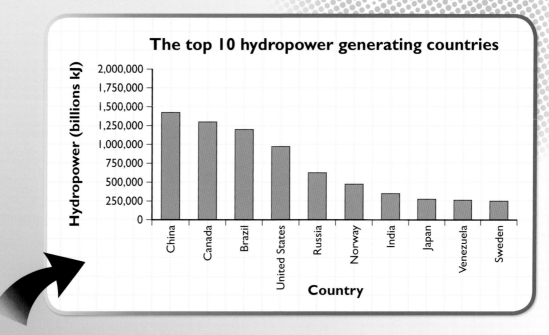

The top 10 hydropower generating countries

Bar charts

A bar chart is good for comparing groups. These groups do not necessarily affect each other. For example, information about the top 10 hydroelectricity-producing countries is best shown as a bar graph, because each country is separate. From the graph we can immediately see which countries produce the most hydroelectricity per day.

Stacked bar charts

A stacked bar chart provides more information than a simple bar chart. Each bar in a stacked bar chart is like a rectangular pie chart. It makes it easy to compare different sets of percentages.

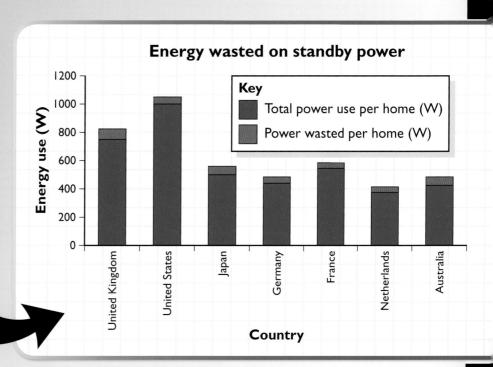

Energy wasted on standby power

Key
Total power use per home (W)
Power wasted per home (W)

GLOSSARY

Asia Pacific area covering several countries: coastal East Asia, Southeast Asia, New Zealand, Australia, Papua New Guinea, and neighboring islands in the Pacific Ocean

atmosphere layer of gases around Earth

atom tiny particle. All things are made up of atoms.

chemical plant industrial place that produces chemicals

climate general type of weather an area has over a period of time

data information, often in the form of numbers

deposit pocket of oil or gas trapped in rocks

developed country country where many people are relatively wealthy and work in offices or in new technology, rather than producing food or raw materials

developing country country where most people have little money and work either on farms or in industries producing raw materials

energy-efficient describes a machine or device that uses less energy to do a job than other similar machines or devices

former Soviet Union former communist country spanning eastern Europe and northern Asia

fossil fuel coal, oil, or natural gas. These are all fuels that are found in the ground and have taken millions of years to form.

fuel substance that can be burned or used in some other way to produce energy

generator machine that produces electricity

goods things people buy and sell in stores

ice sheet large, very thick layer of ice completely covering an area of land or sea

insulated if something is insulated, heat cannot easily get into or out of it

kinetic energy energy of movement

lubricant substance used to reduce friction

megawatt (one megawatt=one million watts) unit used for measuring power

mine large underground hole for getting natual minerals such as coal

oil refinery industrial place where the unwanted elements are removed from oil

potential energy stored energy

proportion size of a group of data compared to other groups, or to the whole set of data

radioactive giving out invisible waves of radiation or streams of microscopic particles. Exposure to radioactivity can harm humans.

recycle make something new from old materials that have already been used

renewable energy source of energy, such as wind or solar energy, that will not run out

turbine many-bladed fan or a propeller

x-axis horizontal line on a graph

y-axis vertical line on a graph

Books

Arnold, Nick. *Horrible Science: Killer Energy and Shocking Electricity*. New York: Scholastic, 2006.

Green, Jen. *Why Should I Save Energy?* Hauppauge, N.Y. : Barron's Educational Series, 2005.

Parker, Steve. *Green Files: Future Power*. Chicago: Heinemann Library, 2004.

Saunders, Nigel, and Steven Chapman. *Energy Essentials: Renewable Energy*. Chicago: Raintree, 2005.

Websites

The website for the National Center for Education Statistics has a section in which you can create different graphs.
http://nces.ed.gov/nceskids/createagraph

The Energy Information Administration has facts, games, history, and related links on its website.
www.eia.doe.gov/kids

Energy Quest is the California Energy Commission's website. There is a lot of information on different types of energy here.
www.energyquest.ca.gov

The U.S. Department of Energy's website has information about fossil fuels.
http://fossil.energy.gov/education/energylessons

INDEX